THE *Carluccio's* COLLECTION

BAKING

ANTONIO & PRISCILLA CARLUCCIO

Dedicated to the memory of
photographer André Martin

Quadrille
PUBLISHING

Contents

All recipes in the book are for 4 people unless otherwise
stated. Use either all metric or all imperial measures, as
the two are not necessarily interchangeable.

Foreword

It is certainly not a coincidence that some of the rites of the Catholic Church are centred around bread, which is given to people as a representation of something pure – of life itself. In fact bread has been the symbol and basic food of Western Society for the last four or five thousand years, just as rice has been for Eastern cultures.

The first culture in which bread was made with the available grains was that of the Egyptians, around three or two thousand years BC. The available flours were milled from millet, spelt and hard grains, giving a flat unleavened bread, probably because of the lack of a raising agent. It must have been the bread-makers of that time who once left some dough in a corner and saw with great amazement that its volume had doubled. It is from that point that the bread-making that we know today started, producing bread that was soft and no longer tooth-breaking.

During a short holiday staying at the resort of Macugnaga in Northern Italy at the foot of Monte Rosa, where the Walser culture originated on the other side of the mountain in the Swiss Valliser region, I discovered a locally made bread that was apparently baked once a year. This bread is very black in appearance and is made with a mixture of whole flour of different grains; it is extremely hard and only edible in soups or milk or if it is left to soften in water. In most of the remote side valleys of the Alps, similar breads exist alongside contemporary bread.

The Italians like to eat lots of bread and baked foods in general. From the central baking oven that stood in the village fifty or sixty years ago to the outside wood-fired oven in which country people used to bake all sorts of foods, to the super-modern individual ovens present in every household, all of them are used at least once a week to bake all sorts of things. Although industrial technology has become predominant in the production of bread and other food for the masses, Italians are now opting more and more for the infinitely superior quality of bread produced by the many bakers who are returning to the good old methods. Italian baking is very varied, because every region offers real artisanal bread made according to their own historical traditions and tasting quite unique and absolutely delicious. This nostalgic return to the 'good old days' (never mind that the goods are more expensive!) guarantees that you are eating something of quality.

I still remember when I used to pass by the semi-closed door of a bakery early in the morning, attracted by the smell of fresh bread, and saw the baker whistling his favourite song and baking the goods that found their way on to tables later on in the day. In Turin they used to prepare crispy and long hand-drawn *grissini*, while in Liguria a fabulous *focaccia* flavoured with olive oil comes out of the oven ready to eat. In Tuscany they bake the only unsalted bread in Italy for use in the famous *bruschetta* of toasted bread dribbled with extra-virgin olive oil. In the South, in areas like Puglia and Sicily, they prefer a more substantial bread made with durum wheat semolina to accompany their strongly flavoured dishes. Sardinia offers perhaps the most peculiar bread ever – the *pane carasau* or the *carta di musica* as they call it locally. Baked to last for months, it is only a couple of millimetres thick and can be eaten in soups, by itself or softened in water and then rolled and stuffed and grilled with cheese and ham.

However, Naples can be justly claim its position as the capital of baking, since no one can ignore their creation, the pizza – which has conquered the world. The Neapolitan ovens also bake the famous *pastiera di grano* – a cake made with whole-grain wheat and ricotta cheese.

The joy of cooking with an oven (incidentally, one of the few methods of cooking where your attention is not constantly required), can be remarkable. I would suggest that you start to learn to cook more with an oven – be it bread, cakes, biscuits or tarts, all require just a good choice of ingredients and good preparation. You will take great satisfaction from seeing your guests enjoying the results of your labours.

Antonio Carluccio

Bread and Baking Ingredients

The following items are those basic ingredients from which most baked goods are made – grains, binders, fats and raising agents:

Burro / Butter

Butter is obtained by collecting the cream off the top of the milk. After allowing the cream to undergo a little natural fermentation to develop flavour, it is put in a revolving container and churned until a clotted mass of the fat results, and the excess water discarded. This mass is then pressed into rectangular shapes for packaging.

Italian butter is generally unsalted and is especially flavoursome, particularly when made with Alpine milk. Butter is very much used in the making of cakes, biscuits and tarts, but is used in general cooking mainly in the North. Even there nowadays, however, it is suffering in competition with Southern olive oil for reasons of health. Butter is the dairy product with the highest fat content, at least 82 per cent, and highly saturated.

Farina / Flour

This generic term, probably derived from *farro* (spelt), denotes the product of milling any dry seed, grain or pulse. While the word *farina* on its own is only used to describe wheat flour, other ground grains are described in the same way, hence *farina di mais* (cornflour or polenta), *farina di orzo* (pearl barley flour), etc.

With the addition of liquid and spices, flour was found to be an endlessly versatile ingredient that could be made into pasta, bread, biscuits, or used as a thickening for sauces and soups. Flour is graded by its fineness and its suitability for different types of cooking: farina 00 (*doppio zero*) is used for fresh pasta and cakes; tipo 0 for bread.

Frumento / Tender Wheat

This cereal belongs to the *Triticum* genus, of which *farro* is also a member. This variety of wheat is a tender grain. It is densely cultivated in the extensive Po Valley, where it is popularly used to make bread.

Lardo / Lard

Fresh lard is taken from the fatty sides of a pig when the meat is butchered. It is then soaked in brine and hung for a few months before being used in cooking.

Lievito / Raising Agent

There are two types of yeast, one natural and one synthetic. They both have the task, through their fermentation, of producing bubbles in the combination of flour and water, or other ingredients, in order to raise and aerate the mixture and thus obtain a softness in baked goods. Bread without yeast would be flat and hard and inedible.

The best yeast is brewer's yeast, a by-product of making beer. The pinky brown substance is diluted with water and mixed with whatever is to be baked. It is important to allow the fermentation to take place in a warm place, before putting the dough in a hot oven. Synthetic yeast does not need any such pre-fermentation.

Uova / Eggs

Eggs are among the most versatile of ingredients, which apart from their obvious myriad uses boiled, scrambled, poached and fried, are employed in all manner of preparations, like cakes, breads, biscuits, custards and ice-creams, for their enriching and binding properties.

Mostaccioli (must biscuits, see page 59) served with Marsala wine in a café in Erice, Sicily.

Making Bread

A range of Sicilian breads in a baker's tray.

Basic Crusty White Bread

650 g (1 lb 7 oz) type 00 (doppio zero) tender flour, plus more
for dusting
350 g (12 oz) type 0 or strong bread flour
25 g (¾ oz) salt
15–30 g (½–1 oz) fresh brewer's yeast
15 g (½ oz) malt extract

Sift both the flours, the salt and the yeast into the bowl of a food
processor. Add 550 ml (19 fl oz) water at 30°C (86°F) and process to a
smooth dough, adding a, little more water if necessary to obtain
smooth dough. Add the malt extract and process briefly to
incorporate.

Turn out on a floured surface, knead for about 10 minutes, until
elastic, then place in a bowl, cover and leave to rise in a warm place for
1 hour or until doubled in size.

Divide the dough into 6 pieces and shape each into a loaf (in a loaf
tin if you prefer). Leave each to rise for a further 30 minutes.

Preheat the oven to 230°C/450°F/gas8. Bake the loaves for 40–45
minutes, until their bases sound hollow when tapped.

Makes 6 loaves

Signor Garello, the baker in Turin's Via Maddalena.

Focaccia

FOCACCIA

30 g (1 oz) fresh yeast
about 175 ml (6 fl oz) lukewarm water
500 g (1 lb 1½ oz) type 00 (doppio zero) flour
2 tbsp olive oil, plus extra for the baking tray and for drizzling
pinch of salt
25 g (¾ oz) coarse salt

Dissolve the yeast in the water. Put the flour in a bowl, then add the oil, yeast liquid and pinch of salt. Mix together, adding more water if necessary to obtain a very soft and smooth dough. Knead for about 10 minutes, until elastic, then place in a bowl, cover and leave to rise in a warm place for 1 hour or until doubled in size.

Preheat the oven to 200°C/400°F/gas6. Lightly oil a large baking tray. Knock back the dough, then dip your fingertips in olive oil and gently press out the very elastic dough until it covers the whole tray. It should be about 2 cm (¾ inch) high. Brush with olive oil and then make small indentations here and there in the dough with your finger-tips. Sprinkle the coarse salt over the top and bake for 25–30 minutes, until a golden-brown crust has formed. As soon as the bread comes out of the oven, drizzle more olive oil on top; this will be absorbed, giving a wonderful flavour.

Allow to cool, then cut into squares and enjoy. It can be eaten plain or, as they do in Genoa, made into a sandwich with some mortadella while still warm!
Serves 6-8

Focaccia / Flat Bread

Focaccia is eaten on its own as a snack and used to make sandwiches, when it is particularly good filled with mortadella. *Focaccia* has given rise to the pizza in Naples and the savoury and sweet version of pizza, pinza, *in Veneto and Emilia-Romagna, using polenta flour.*

There are a huge number of different varieties of focaccia, *including the* smacafam *from Trentino, using buckwheat flour. The dough has onions in it and is topped with sausage meat. The Calabrian* pitta *is similar to Middle-Eastern bread, except that it is formed into a ring, cut open and filled, while still hot, with* ciccioli *(pork fat), oil and chilli or grated pecorino. In Lombardy, they make* fitascetta, *topped with a jam of red onions and salt or sugar, while the Tuscans make* stiacciata, *a proved dough that is mixed with sugar, eggs and spices before being baked. Finally, the Ligurian speciality, known variously as* pizzalandrea *or* pissadella, *and* sardenaria *in Genovese, is related to the French onion tart,* pissaladière.

Casatiello

SAVOURY EASTER BREAD

**Casatiello, Casatello /
Neapolitan Easter Bread**

*Together with Pastiera di Grano (see page
48) this special savoury bread is made in
Naples for Easter, usually in batches of two
or three, so there are always spare loaves to
give as presents to friends. Every family
has its own recipe, but the decoration never
varies – the Easter symbol of the eggs
pushed into the dough before baking. The
eggs are shelled after baking and eaten
with the bread.*

**225 g (8 oz) soft lard (you could use butter, but lard gives an
 authentic taste)**

100 g (3½ oz) hard pecorino cheese, grated

100 g (3½ oz) parmesan cheese, grated

100 g (3½ oz) provolone cheese, very finely grated

100 g (3½ oz) neapolitan sausage, cut into very small cubes

1 tbsp freshly ground black pepper, not too fine

1 tsp salt

8 eggs

FOR THE DOUGH:

600 g (1 lb 5 oz) type 00 (doppio zero) flour

60 g (2 oz) soft lard

55 g (1¾ oz) fresh yeast

200 ml (7 fl oz) lukewarm water

To make the dough, put the flour in a bowl and rub in the lard. Dissolve
the yeast in the water, add to the flour and mix well to form a dough.
Knead for 10–15 minutes, until soft and silky, then put in a bowl, cover
with a cloth and leave for about 2 hours, until doubled in size.

Knock back the risen dough and knead it briefly to eliminate air
bubbles. Flatten it into a rectangle about 3 cm (1¼ inches) thick, dot
half the lard, cheeses and sausage over it and sprinkle with half the
pepper and salt. Fold up the bottom third of dough, then fold down the
top third and knead to distribute the ingredients and work in the lard.
Flatten it into a rectangle again and cover with the remaining lard,
cheeses and sausage, then repeat the folding and kneading. Place the
dough in a greased 25-cm (10-inch) ring mould for the traditional

effect, or lay it on a greased baking tray in a ring shape or divide it into 2
or 4 smaller loaves, then cover and leave to rise for another 2 hours.

Preheat the oven to 190°C/375°F/gas5. Wash the eggs and push them
half way into the dough. Bake for 1 hour, then remove from the oven and
leave to cool. It can be kept for a few days.

Serves 8

Torta Pasqualina

EASTER TART

4 tbsp olive oil, plus more for the tart pan

2 onions, thinly sliced

hearts of 8 fresh very young artichokes

675 g (1½ lb) shortcrust pastry

6 eggs

100 g (3½ oz) parmesan cheese

salt and pepper

800 g (1¾ lb) spinach, blanched and coarsely chopped

Torta Pasqualina / Easter tart

This is another traditional savoury Italian Easter treat, this time from Liguria. It is based on pastry, vegetables and eggs, and is eaten especially on Easter Monday, Pasquetta, when almost everybody goes for a picnic. My mother used to make it quite often, however, regardless of tradition.

Heat the oil in a heavy-based pan and fry the onions until soft. Add the artichoke hearts with a glass of water, cover and braise very gently until tender.

Preheat the oven to 180°C/350°F/gas4 and oil a 25-cm (10-inch) tart pan. Roll out the pastry and use to line the pan.

In a bowl, lightly beat the eggs. Add the parmesan cheese, with salt and pepper to taste. Add the spinach, and the artichokes and onions. Mix well.

Fill the pastry shell with the artichoke mixture and bake in the oven for 40 minutes. Serve hot or cold.

Serves 8

There are probably as many versions of this savoury Ligurian tart, traditionally made at Easter, as there are families in the region.

Panpepato

PEPPERED BREAD

85 g (3 oz) almonds, blanched, skinned, toasted and chopped

85 g (3 oz) hazelnuts, toasted and skinned

85 g (3 oz) walnut halves

55 g (1¾ oz) pine nuts

55 g (1¾ oz) Muscat raisins, left to soak in a few tablespoons of
    vin santo for 30 minutes, then drained

60 g (2 oz) bitter cocoa powder

100 g (3½ oz) mixed candied peel, cut into small cubes

½ tsp each ground cinnamon and ground coriander

½ tsp freshly grated nutmeg

1 tsp freshly ground black pepper

125 g (4½ oz) acacia honey

plain flour, to bind

butter for greasing the tray

Preheat the oven to 160°C/325°F/gas3. Mix all the ingredients together
in a bowl, adding enough flour to obtain a fairly stiff mixture. Shape
with wet hands into a round loaf and place on a buttered baking tray.

    Bake for 30 minutes, then leave to cool before serving.

Makes 1 loaf (serves 6-8)

Versions of this cake exist in different regions but

principally Tuscany. This recipe, however, comes

from a pâtisserie in the Umbrian town of Gubbio.

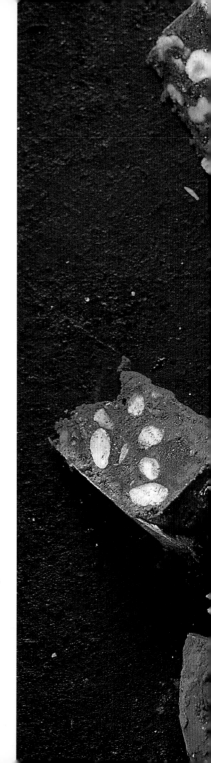

Panpepato / Peppered Bread

Panpepato *is a sweet bread that is made in a number of Italian regions and was the predecessor of Tuscan* panforte. *It gets its name from the addition of copious amounts of ground black pepper to the more usual ingredients of almonds, hazelnuts, walnuts, pine nuts, candied orange and lime peel, wheat flour and honey. The bread is then cooked in a medium oven for 40 minutes and allowed to cool. Sometimes the loaf is also covered in a layer of dark chocolate.*

Pizzette Margherita

LITTLE MOZZARELLA AND TOMATO PIZZAS

500 g (1 lb) tomato pulp or blended chopped tomatoes

400 g (14 oz) mozzarella, thinly sliced

20 basil leaves

salt and pepper

FOR THE DOUGH:

25 g (¾ oz) fresh yeast

200 ml (7 fl oz) lukewarm water

500 g (1 lb 1½ oz) type 00 (doppio zero) flour

3 tbsp extra-virgin olive oil, plus more for drizzling

1 tsp salt

½ tsp sugar

Pizza

It is not difficult to prepare an original pizza provided you have the right ingredients, the know-how and a good oven. This type of focaccia has been developed by the Neapolitans, thanks to their imaginative way of using the best local ingredients – the good flour, good water, good tomatoes, good basil, good mozzarella cheese and good olive oil.

Make the dough: dissolve yeast in the water. Pile flour, make a well in the centre and add oil, salt and sugar. Slowly incorporate yeast mixture, then knead dough with fingers and palm until soft and silky. Put in a bowl, dust with flour, cover and leave to rise for 1 hour or until doubled in size.

Knock back the dough, divide it into 12–16 pieces, then knead each piece briefly and reshape it into a ball. Cover and leave to rise for 15 minutes. Preheat the oven to 220°C/425°F/gas7.

Flatten each ball of dough a little with a rolling pin, then stretch it out with your fingertips until it is about 12.5 cm (5 inches) in diameter and slightly thicker at the edges. Place on 2 or 4 oiled baking trays. Spread the tomato over the pizza bases, then distribute the mozzarella over the top. Sprinkle with salt and drizzle with extra-virgin olive oil. Bake for about 8–10 minutes, then sprinkle over the basil leaves and some coarsely ground black pepper and serve straight away.

Makes 12-16

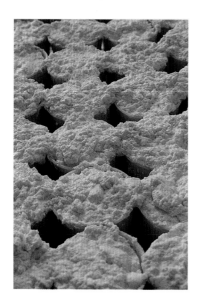

Torta Rustica di Ricotta

SAVOURY RICOTTA CAKE

Torta Rustica di Ricotta

Ricotta is a wonderful vehicle for both sweet and savoury flavours. It is very convenient because it is also fairly low in fat and mixes perfectly with eggs to produce a delightful and not too heavy result. My mother used to conceal any leftover salami and cheese in this savoury ricotta cake. It was our favourite!

25 g (¾ oz) butter

3 tbsp breadcrumbs

500 g (1 lb 1½ oz) very fresh ricotta cheese, preferably sheep's-milk ricotta

4 eggs, separated

45 g (1½ oz) parmesan cheese, grated

55 g (1¾ oz) plain flour

salt and pepper

100 g (3½ oz) mixed melting cheeses, such as provolone, pecorino, scamorza, etc, cut into very small cubes

100 g (3½ oz) Parma ham, salami, speck, etc, very finely chopped

Preheat the oven to 200°C/400°F/gas6. Use the butter to grease a 20-cm (8-inch) ovenproof dish and dust with the breadcrumbs.

Put the ricotta in a bowl. Beat the egg yolks with the parmesan cheese, flour, a little salt and plenty of freshly ground black pepper. Fold this mixture into the ricotta and then add the cheese and ham.

Beat the egg whites until stiff and fold them gently into the ricotta mixture until it is smooth and light. Pour it into the prepared dish, smooth the top level and bake for 30–40 minutes or until a nice crust has formed.

Turn out on to a serving dish and eat warm. It is also good cold. Serves 6

Taralli

SAVOURY BISCUITS

500 g (1 lb 1½ oz) type 0 flour
125 g (4½ oz) lard
55 g (2 oz) brewer's yeast
2 tbsp fennel seeds
crushed dried chillies to taste
salt and pepper
extra-virgin olive oil

Mix the flour with the lard, yeast and spices. Season with salt and pepper. Add enough water to make a workable dough, then mix again until all the ingredients are well blended. Take small pieces of the dough and shape each one into a small sausage. Then join all of them together to form a circle. Sprinkle with oil and place on a baking tray to rise for an hour or so.

Preheat the oven to 150°C/300°F/gas2. Bake the biscuits for 1 hour. Allow them to cool, when they become crumbly and dry.
Makes about 20

Taralli

This round savoury biscuit was traditionally made in Campania, but from there it spread to Puglia, then Calabria and finally Sicily.
It is loved for its flavour and crunchiness, as well as for the fact that it is so easy to make and can keep so well in an airtight jar.

This crumbly round savoury biscuit, traditionally made in Campania and Puglia, can be eaten on its own as a snack and is often served to accompany antipasti.

Prussiani

SWEET PUFF PASTRY BISCUITS

Prussiani

These delicious little puff pastry biscuits are traditionally served at breakfast or with morning coffee. Puff pastry is one of those recipes that is so difficult that it is seldom made at home; it is more likely to be the ultimate challenge in baking. However, the results are so much better than what may be achieved with commercially produced puff pastry – which always uses an inferior fat rather than good tasty butter – that it is worth the effort.

500 g (1 lb 1½ oz) plain flour
pinch of salt
175 g (6 oz) block of hard butter
10 generous handfuls of sugar

Put the flour and salt into a large bowl with 250 ml (9 fl oz) water and mix well to produce a dough. On a floured surface, roll the dough out to form a square just over twice the size of the block of butter.

Place butter in the middle of one side of pastry square. Fold over other half and press down edges with a rolling pin to seal package around butter. Turn package so fold is to one side and roll out to form rectangle three times as long as it is wide. Fold bottom third up and top third down over that. Again seal the edges with a rolling pin. Wrap loosely in cling film and chill for an hour. Repeat rolling, folding and chilling 4 or 5 times more, each time giving pastry a quarter turn clockwise before beginning.

Preheat oven to 200°C/400°F/gas6. Sprinkle handful of sugar over work surface, place chilled pastry on it and sprinkle more sugar over it. Roll out into a square, sprinkling more sugar as you roll. Fold over in half and then fold this in half. Roll again, sprinkling with more sugar as you go, into a long rectangular shape. Fold this rectangle in half and repeat rolling and folding once more. Roll again into a rectangle, then fold lengthwise to form a 'sausage'. Slice into 1-cm (½-inch) thick circles.

Place on a baking tray well spaced apart. Bake for 12 minutes, then turn the biscuits over and bake for a further 5 minutes.
Makes 24–30

Clockwise from the top: sfogliatelli (page 62), tiny babas, prussiani, tiny sfogliatelli.

Cantucci

TUSCAN ALMOND BISCUITS

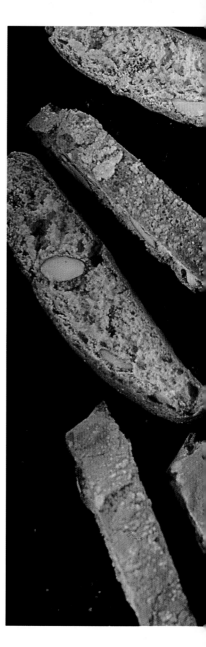

300 g (10½ oz) caster sugar
4 eggs, plus 3 more egg yolks
500 g (1 lb 1½ oz) type 00 (doppio zero) flour
200 g (7 oz) unpeeled almonds, lightly toasted
pinch of salt
1 tsp orange essence
1 tsp bicarbonate of soda or baking powder
butter, for greasing

Preheat the oven to 190°C/375°F/gas 5.

Beat the caster sugar with 3 of the eggs and the 3 extra egg yolks until you have a well-amalgamated foam. Add the flour, almonds, salt, orange essence and bicarbonate of soda or baking powder. Mix gently until you have a soft dough. Divide into longish sausages and place on a buttered baking tray, pressing each one until it is flattened to about 2 cm (¾ inch) high and 4 cm (1½ inch) wide. Make sure the dough sausages are spaced far enough apart to give them room to rise as they bake. Lightly beat the remaining egg and brush each one with a little of this glaze.

Bake for 15 minutes. Remove from the oven and cut each biscuit diagonally into 2-cm (¾-inch) wide strips and return to the oven until completely cooked and dry, about 10 minutes.

Remove from the oven and allow to cool, before storing in an airtight jar or tin until needed.

Makes about 24

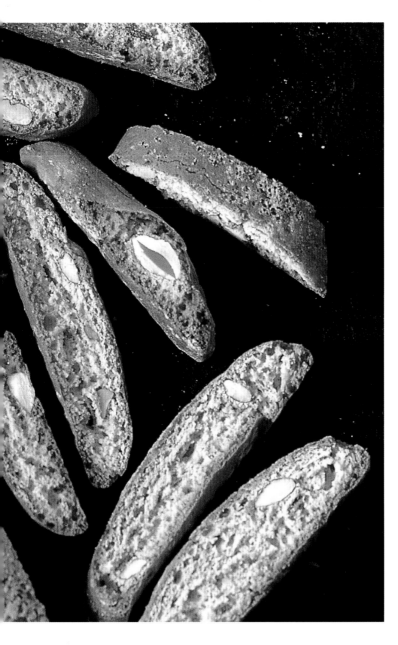

Vin Santo

This rich aromatic Tuscan wine is a delicious dessert wine, traditionally used to dip Cantucci *biscuits after a meal. Some attribute the use of the word* santo *here to the fact that this wine is used sometimes for celebration of the Mass, others because the wine originated from Xantos in Greece. It is produced from Malvasia and Trebbiano grapes which, after harvesting, are put on straw mats to dry to increase the sugar content before being turned into wine. Depending upon the fermentation, the ageing process in wooden casks for at least 3 years produces a wine that may be sweet, semi-sweet or dry. Vin Santo is also used as a flavouring in pastries and creams.*

Amaretti
ALMOND BISCUITS

275 g (10 oz) sweet almonds

30 g (1 oz) bitter almonds, blanched and skinned, then toasted until
    dry but not coloured

500 g (1 lb) icing sugar

whites of 4 eggs

55 g (1¾ oz) caster sugar

Preheat the oven to 220°C/425°F/gas7. Reduce the sweet and bitter almonds to a coarse flour either with a pestle and mortar or in a food processor. Gradually incorporate the icing sugar and egg whites until you obtain a firm mixture. Roll this with your hands to a sausage shape about 3 cm (1¼ inches) in diameter and cut it into slices 1 cm (½ inch) thick.

Place well spaced apart on a buttered baking sheet. Sprinkle with the caster sugar and bake for about 15 minutes, until pale brown and crunchy. Leave to cool on the baking sheet.

Makes about 40

Amaretto

There are many varieties of this popular biscuit, the most well-known being the crispy amaretto di saronno, *a pair of small amaretti wrapped in paper and served with coffee in almost every Italian restaurant or trattoria. It takes its name from the town of Saronno, where it has been made for the last hundred years by Lazzaroni.* Amaretti *can be found all over Italy, however, ranging in texture from dry and crisp to moist and soft.*

There are two versions of these famous little almond biscuits. One is for soft amaretti and the other, this recipe, for dry and crumbly ones.

Ricciarelli

TUSCAN ALMOND BISCUITS

300 g (10½ oz) freshly ground sweet almonds
350 g (12 oz) sugar
grated zest of 1 lemon
1 tsp vanilla sugar or a few drops of vanilla essence
beaten whites of 2 eggs
1 tbsp honey
icing sugar, for dusting

Preheat oven to 190°C/375°F/gas5. Mix almonds and sugar, and work thoroughly before adding the lemon zest, vanilla, egg whites and honey. Mix again to incorporate all the ingredients, then roll dough on a surface dusted with icing sugar, until it is 2 cm (¾ inch) thick. Using an oval cutter or knife, cut out lozenges 4–5 cm (1½–2 inches) in length. Place on a baking tray lined with rice paper also covered with a 3 mm (⅛ inch) layer of icing sugar.

Bake for 20 minutes, but don't let biscuits brown. Makes 40

This speciality of Sienna is a biscuit made with almonds and dusted with a large amount of icing sugar. They can be bought ready-made, but the home-made version is so much better.

Savoiardi

SPONGE FINGERS

6 eggs, separated
125 g (4½ oz) caster sugar
150 g (5 oz) type 00 (doppio zero) flour, sifted
30 g (1 oz) icing sugar
1½ sachets of vanilla sugar
25 g (¾ oz) granulated sugar

Preheat the oven to 180°C/350°F/gas4. Beat the egg yolks with the caster sugar until the mixture is very thick and mousse-like. Gradually fold in the flour. In a separate bowl, beat the egg whites until stiff, then sift in the icing sugar and carefully but thoroughly fold it in. Fold this into the egg yolk mixture together with the vanilla sugar, being careful not to knock air out of the mixture.

Put it into a piping bag and pipe on to a buttered baking sheet in little sausage shapes about 12.5 cm (5 inches) long and 3 cm (1¼ inches) wide, spacing them well apart. Sprinkle with the granulated sugar and bake for about 18 minutes. They should be dry and a wonderful golden colour.

Leave to cool on a wire rack, then store them in an airtight container.
Makes 400g (14 oz)

Vanilla Sugar

You can make your own vanilla sugar very easily simply by placing one or two vanilla pods in a jar with some sugar and leaving them for several days until the sugar absorbs the flavour. The other advantage is that the pods may be used for dishes which call for their use and then dried off and returned to the sugar to keep on doing their good work.

You can buy a special baking tin for these light and spongy little biscuits, which gives a deeper, more regular shape. They can also just be piped out on to a baking tray. They are ideal for making *tiramisu* and *zuppa inglese*.

Panforte

TRADITIONAL TUSCAN CAKE

250 g (9 oz) almonds, blanched, skinned and toasted

150 g (5 oz) walnuts or pecan nuts

55 g (1¾ oz) candied cedro (citron peel), cut into small strips

250 g (9 oz) candied pumpkin, cut into small chunks

2 tsp ground cinnamon

2 tsp ground coriander seeds

½ tsp freshly grated nutmeg

200 g (7 oz) plain flour

200 g (7 oz) icing sugar

200 g (7 oz) honey (acacia is best)

a few sheets of rice paper

2 tbsp vanilla sugar

Preheat the oven to 160°C/325°F/gas3. Mix the almonds, walnuts or pecans, candied peel, pumpkin and spices together in a bowl. Add the flour and mix in very well.

Put the icing sugar, honey and a tablespoon of water in a heavy-based pan and heat gently until dissolved. Increase the heat so that the mixture bubbles and then stir with a wooden spoon until it forms a dense, pale-brown caramel. Pour it on to the flour and nuts and mix until smooth.

Use the rice paper to line a 20-cm (8-inch) cake tin, 4 cm (1½ inches) deep. Spread the mixture in it, levelling the top with a spatula. Bake in the oven for about 30 minutes, then remove and leave to cool in the tin. Dust with the vanilla sugar. It can be kept for a long time but I doubt you will be able to!

Serves 10

Torta di Nocciole e Cioccolato

HAZELNUT AND CHOCOLATE CAKE

300 g (10½ oz) butter, melted, plus more for the cake tin

375 g (13 oz) type 00 (doppio zero) flour, plus more for dusting

300 g (10½ oz) hazelnuts, toasted and skinned

6 eggs

500 g (1 lb) caster sugar

2 tsp baking powder

150 ml (¼ pint) milk

100 g (3½ oz) bitter chocolate (at least 70% cocoa solids), cubed small

Chocolate

Italy is quite famous for good chocolate, the industry and artisans are spread in all the regions and they mostly use the best-quality cocoa beans from Ecuador, the Ivory Coast and Ghana. A company in Turin, Peyrano, still imports the cocoa beans and makes the very lengthy transformation to produce bars of cioccolato or cioccolatini (small chocolates), with the addition of all sorts of flavourings, such as orange, mint, vanilla and many more.

Preheat the oven to 180°C/350°F/gas4 and butter and flour a 25-cm (10-inch) cake tin.

Put the hazelnuts in a food processor and reduce to a coarse flour. Using an electric mixer, beat the eggs with the sugar and baking powder until the mixture is mousse-like and thick enough to leave a trail on the surface when drizzled from the beaters. Gently but thoroughly fold in the melted butter and milk, then fold in the flour and hazelnuts, followed by the chocolate.

Pour the mixture into the prepared cake tin and bake for 45 minutes, or until a skewer inserted in the centre comes out dry. Leave to cool before serving.

Serves 6-8

I can't resist any hazelnut cake. I find the taste of the nuts, especially roasted, highly seductive. I think you will agree.

Castagnaccio

CHESTNUT CAKE

750 g (1¾ lb) fresh chestnut flour

pinch of salt

6 tbsp caster sugar

6 tbsp virgin olive oil

3–4 sprigs of rosemary

150 g (5 oz) zibibbo raisins or ordinary raisins

Preheat the oven to 180°C/350°F/gas4. Mix the chestnut flour, salt and caster sugar with enough cold water to obtain a soft but not too runny mixture.

Put the olive oil in a deep 30 x 40 cm (12 x 16 inch) baking tray and spread evenly, then pour in the chestnut batter. Sprinkle with the rosemary and raisins.

Bake for 20 minutes, until golden. Cut into squares to serve. It's best served hot but can also be eaten cold.

Serves 8-10

Chestnut Flour

Ground dried chestnuts can be made into a flour which is used to make Castagnaccio *as here, for the thickening of soups, and is sometimes mixed with wheat flour in the making of certain types of pasta. Chestnut flour is also mixed with water, sugar and vanilla to make* crema di castagne, *a filling for sweet ravioli.*

There exist various versions of this seasonal dish, which is made with the flour of new autumn chestnuts. This is the one of the simplest and tastiest ways of cooking it.

Croccante di Nocciole

HAZELNUT CRUNCH

400 g (14 oz) caster sugar
100 g (3½ oz) honey
zest of 2 tangerines, cut into strips, then into very small dice
500 g (1 lb) hazelnuts, toasted and skinned
a few sheets of rice paper
1 lemon, cut in half

Melt the sugar and honey in a heavy-based pan over a gentle heat. Raise the heat slightly and, when the sugar begins to go a blondish-brown colour, add the tangerine zest. Stir for a minute with a wooden spoon, then add the hazelnuts. Heat a little, stirring, until the hazelnuts are coated with the sugar syrup.

Pour the very hot mixture on to the rice paper and use the lemon halves to spread it out to about 2.5 cm (1 inch) thick (lemons are used because they don't stick to the mixture). As soon as it has cooled down but is still warm, cut into cubes with a large knife. They will still be attached at the bottom. Wait until they are completely cold, then break the cubes apart. Put them in an airtight jar and enjoy them when you feel like it. At Christmas they are served at the end of the meal.
Makes about 1 kg (2lb 3oz)

Hazelnut

In Piedmont, the best hazelnuts are roasted then ground into an extremely fine paste to make nougat and Gianduiotti chocolate, while in Campania they are used to make this Croccante di Nocciole. They are also used in a huge number of biscuits and cakes all over the country.

This is a popular sweet at every village *festa* (fête), especially in the South. It can be made with almonds, pistachios or mixed nuts.

Crostata di Cugna

MIXED FRUIT JAM TART

500 g (1 lb 1½ oz) 00 (doppio zero) flour
200 g (7 oz) soft butter, cut into small cubes
5 egg yolks
200 g (7 oz) caster sugar
1 tbsp vanilla sugar
grated zest of ½ lemon
pinch of salt
350 g (12 oz) favourite mixed fruit jam

Pile the flour up on a work surface into a volcano shape, make a well in the centre and add the butter, 4 of the egg yolks, the caster sugar, vanilla sugar, lemon zest and salt. Gradually draw in the flour and then with the palm of your hand knead quickly and lightly to obtain a smooth dough. Wrap in cling film and leave to rest in the refrigerator for about 1 hour.

Preheat the oven to 180°C/350°F/gas4. Take three-quarters of the pastry and roll it out on a lightly floured board until it is large enough to fit a 25-cm (10-inch) round flan tin or a rectangular baking tray. Butter the tin or baking tray and line with the pastry, trimming off the excess. Fill with the jam, then roll out the remaining pastry and cut it into long strips with a pastry wheel or a sharp knife to make a lattice for the tart. Brush with the remaining egg yolk and bake for 30 minutes. Leave to cool and then serve.

Serves 6-8

Pastiera di Grano

WHOLE WHEAT TART

FOR THE PASTRY:

150 g (5 oz) caster sugar

150 g (5 oz) butter or cooking fat, plus more for the
pan

yolks of 3 large eggs

300 g (10½ oz) flour

FOR THE FILLING:

200 g (7 oz) whole wheat, or 500 g (1 lb) canned
cooked wheat (called gran pastiera)

500 ml (18 fl oz) milk (if using fresh whole wheat)

grated zest of 1 lemon

1 tsp ground cinnamon

2 tsp vanilla sugar

grated zest of ½ orange

300 g (10½ oz) ricotta cheese

4 large eggs, separated

1 small wine glass of orange flower water

150 g (5 oz) candied peel, finely chopped

225 g (8 oz) caster sugar

icing sugar for dusting

If using fresh whole wheat, 2 days ahead soak it for
24 hours in several changes of water. Next day
simmer the grain in the milk with the zest of half a
lemon for 3 or 4 hours on a very low heat. When it
is cooked (or if using canned), stir in a pinch of
cinnamon, the vanilla sugar and the remaining

lemon zest and the orange zest. Leave overnight for the flavours to mingle.

Make the pastry: in a large bowl, work together the sugar, butter and the eggs until smooth, then add the flour and gradually incorporate to make a smooth pastry. Set aside in a cool place for 1 hour or more.

Preheat the oven to 190°C/375°F/gas5. Grease a 35-cm (14-inch) diameter flan pan with butter or fat.

To finish the filling: beat the ricotta with the egg yolks and the orange water. Add the candied peel and the flavoured grain to the mixture. Beat the egg whites with the sugar until stiff and fold them very gently into the mixture.

Roll out two-thirds of the pastry and use to line the flan pan, covering the bottom and sides with an equal thickness. Pour in the filling. Roll out the remaining pastry and cut it into long strips to form a lattice top for the tart. Bake for about 45 minutes until coloured light golden.

Allow to cool and then dust with icing sugar.
Serves 10

This Easter recipe will probably appear in every book I write, because it is my mother's and has always been traditional in my family.

Cenci

PASTRY RIBBONS

350 g (12 oz) type 00 (doppio zero) flour

45 g (1½ oz) soft butter

45 g (1½ oz) caster sugar

1 sachet of vanilla sugar

2 eggs

pinch of salt

3 tbsp moscato passito or vin santo

200 g (7 oz) icing sugar

olive oil for deep-frying

Sift the flour into a bowl, add the butter, caster sugar, vanilla sugar, eggs, salt and wine and work together to obtain a very smooth dough. Cover and leave to rest for 1 hour.

Using a rolling pin or a pasta machine, roll out the dough until it is 3 mm (⅛ inch) thick. With a serrated pastry wheel, cut it into strips 15–18 cm (6–7 inches) long and 3–4 cm (1¼–1½ inches) wide, then very patiently tie each one in a loose knot.

Deep-fry them in olive oil, a few at a time to allow them to swim well, until golden and crisp, then put them on kitchen paper to drain off excess oil. When cold, pile them up on a tray and dust them abundantly with the icing sugar. They are irresistible!

Serves 8-10

Cenci

Cenci, *meaning 'rags', are usually made for* Carnevale, *which takes place 40 days before* Easter, *but are now available all year* round. *The term is Tuscan, but they can be* found, *with some minor variations, in all* the regions.

They are made from a dough of type 00 *(doppio zero) wheat flour with the addition of butter, sugar, eggs and a little Vin Santo. The pastry is rolled out, then cut into ribbons and deep-fried, possibly in lard (more usual in the South) but also sometimes in olive oil. They are dusted with copious amounts of icing sugar when cool.*

These moreish pastries are supposed to be eaten during Lent.

Bignole

CHOUX BUNS

Bignè, bignole

The term bignè *refers to any cake made with choux pastry, including profiteroles and eclairs among others. Piedmont has moved even closer to France, with the creation of* bignole, *little balls of choux pastry that are usually filled with cream or zabaglione, then partially dipped in glacé icing.*

pinch of salt
200 g (7 oz) butter
300 g (10½ oz) plain flour
6 whole eggs, plus extra 4 egg yolks
30 g (1 oz) sugar
whipped cream or zabaglione (see right), to serve
lemon-flavoured glacé icing, to serve

Put 500 ml (18 fl oz) water in a pan with the salt and butter and place over a high heat. As soon as it comes to the boil, take the pan off the heat and add the flour. Mix well, then leave to cool.

Preheat the oven to 200°C/400°F/gas6. When the contents of the pan are cool, add the whole eggs, extra egg yolks, and the sugar. Mix thoroughly, then place the mixture in an icing bag fitted with a plain nozzle. Pipe small dots of dough on a buttered baking tray.

Bake for about 20 minutes. When done, remove them from the oven and leave to cool. They should have puffed up to 3 or 4 times their initial size and be hollow so they can be filled with cream or zabaglione.

Dip a part of each bignole in a lemon-flavoured glacé icing, leave to set, then serve.

Makes about 24

For a surprise, vary the flavourings – mixing cocoa powder into the filling for some, orange essence for others and lemon zest for the rest.

Zabaglione

Put 16–18 free-range egg yolks,
300 g (10½ oz) caster sugar and
200 ml (7 fl oz) Moscato Passito di
Pantelleria or Marsala in a large bowl
and whisk with a hand-held electric
beater or a whisk until foamy and doubled
in volume.

Put the bowl over a saucepan of gently
simmering water, making sure the water
does not touch the base of the bowl.
Continue to whisk until the mixture is
very thick and has a homogeneous,
creamy but not crumbly texture. It is crucial
not to let it overheat or you will end up
with scrambled eggs. Serve immediately.

For 6–8

Glossary of Bread and Baking

Amaretto / *Macaroon Biscuit*
See page 34.

Anicino / *Anise Biscuit*
These Umbrian biscuits are a testimony to the popularity of aniseed in Italy. The biscuits are a speciality of Orvieto, although they are also made in Sardinia and can be eaten either on their own or dipped in wine like *cantuccini*. In Sardinia they are dipped into the local strong wine, Monica di Sardegna. As a variation, the biscuits can be made with olive oil instead of the usual hard fats, making them tastier and healthier.

Baco di Dama / *Biscuit, Lady's Kiss*
This Piedmontese biscuit gets its name from the fact that the two circles of shortcrust biscuit, sandwiched together with plain chocolate, look like a pair of lips. To make them: mix together 150 g (5 oz) finely ground almonds with 150 g (5 oz) 00 flour, 150 g (5 oz) caster sugar, 150 g (5 oz) soft butter, a little grated lemon, orange or lime zest and 3 egg yolks. Work the mixture until well combined, then form it into little balls and place on a buttered baking tray and bake in an oven preheated to 190°C/375°F/gas5 until golden

brown. Allow the biscuits to cool, then sandwich them together with a little melted chocolate.

Barchetta / *Little Boat, Barquette*
Little boat-shaped biscuits, made from shortcrust pastry, *barchetta* may be filled with fruit, jam or *crema pasticcera* and eaten as a dessert. They can also be filled with shrimps, scrambled egg and caviar, and served as canapés.

Bastone / *Stick, Baguette*
This long stick of white bread is similar to the French baguette (see Pane).

Bignè, Bignole / *Profiterole*
See page 52.

Biova, Biovetta / *Piedmontese Bread*
This Piedmontese bread is now eaten in most of the northern regions of Italy. It is made with *pasta dura*, a hard, unproved dough that is worked well to get rid of air bubbles and to make it softer. The crust of the cooked bread is quite crispy, while the centre is very dense and white. It is often formed and cut into the most incredible shapes, or it can be bought in loaves, the small ones being called *biovetta* and the larger *biova*.

Biscotto / *Biscuit*
Originally a slice of bread, as the name suggests, twice baked to achieve dryness. The *biscotto* was originally a means of conserving bread by drying it, for later reuse by adding moisture again in the form of water or milk (see Frisella). Today the *biscotto* is more a kind of true biscuit, which can be made of eggs and flour with the addition of sugar, honey and yeast and other ingredients like almonds, chocolate, etc, or a combination of these. *Biscotti* can also be savoury, like Taralli or crackers to take the place of bread. *Biscotti* are made both for immediate use or for long keeping, the best examples of each being fresh and dry *amaretti*. Italians use a great deal of *biscotti* of any kind, mostly sweet and mainly to dip into *caffè latte*, the morning breakfast drink.

Buccellato Lucchese / *Lucchese Cake*
This simple cake, looking more like a bread than a cake, is a speciality of Lucca in Tuscany; however, a much more complicated version is made in Sicily, based on eggs and including candied peel. Both cakes are eaten in the same way, though, as dessert or for breakfast, dipped in milk. They keep very well if stored in an airtight tin.

Calzone / *Folded Pizzas*
Calzone, from the word for 'trousers', is made with the same dough as pizzas, and is folded into a pocket around stuffing. The Neapolitans fill theirs with Provolone cheese, mozzarella, hot Neapolitan sausage or salami, all cut into cubes and mixed with beaten eggs. Other recipes include one from Puglia that includes braised sliced onions, ricotta forte, eggs and parmesan; and cooked Swiss chard or spinach with eggs, parmesan and pecorino cheese.

Cannolo / *Filled Sweet Pastry Tube*
Cannoli is probably the best-known Sicilian dessert and gets is name from the fact that it is deep-fried around a piece of cane (*canna*). It used only to be made for *Carnevale* (carnival) and for the feast day of San Carlo. Now it is eaten all year round, not only after meals, but also as a snack. The special pastry is filled with a mixture of ricotta, sugar, candied fruits and chocolate.

Cannoncino / *Little Cannon, Puff Pastry Horn*
A popular pastry in Italy, the pastry horn is made from a rectangular piece of puff pastry, about 30 cm (12 inches) in length and 3–4 cm (1¼ –1½ inches) wide. It is rolled very thin, then wound tightly around a metal cone to make the horn shape. The pastry is then brushed with beaten egg and baked on a buttered baking tray in a hot oven for 20 minutes. When the horns are cool the metal cone is removed and the pastry filled with flavoured creams or zabaglione.

Cantucci, Cantuccini / *Tuscan Almond Biscuits*
See page 32.

Carta da Musica, Pane Carasau / *Flat Sardinian Bread*
This very thin, flat, crispy bread, which resembles old parchment or music manuscript paper (hence its name), is difficult to make and is usually bought now rather than made at home. It is sold in piles of 10 or 20 slices, which are carefully packaged because of their fragility.

Casatiello, Casatello / *Neapolitan Easter Bread*
See page 16.

Cassata
Cassata gets its name from *qus'at*, the Arab word for the small conical container in which the dessert is traditionally made. It used to be made only by nuns during Holy Week, but is now available all year round. There are two versions of the dish, both of which come from Sicily, where it was created. The first is a cake made with marzipan, ricotta and candied fruit; and the second, a later development, made with ice-cream. A smaller version of cassata, called *cassatina*, is often sold in Sicilian bars and cafés.

Cenci, Chiacchere, Bugie / *Pastries*
See page 51.

Ciabatta / *Bread*
One of the most popular breads in Italy and around the world, *ciabatta* is made with type 0 wheat flour and is characterized by its softness and moisture, both of which are due to the long raising time of 6 hours, when the large air holes are formed. Its soft crust is the result of cooking the bread in ovens where water is allowed to evaporate as the bread cooks (see Pane).

Ciambella, Ciambellone, Ciambellina / *Ring-Shaped Cake*
There is a proverb in Italy '*Non tutte le ciambelle riescono con il buco*', which translates as 'not every *ciambella* comes with a hole', meaning not everything can be perfect. The *ciambella* is made from a dough that is baked in a ring mould or simply shaped into a ring. It can be either savoury or sweet, depending on the ingredients added to the basic dough mixture. *Ciambellone* is a larger cake and *ciambellina* a smaller one.

Colomba / *Easter Dove*
This cake, made in the shape of a dove, is an Easter offering representing peace. Like *panettone*, it is now eaten all over Italy and sold abroad in specialist shops. It is quite different to *panettone*, in that

it does not include raisins and has a higher proportion of eggs and butter and includes candied orange peel. It is covered in a sugar-and-almond icing and is eaten as a dessert, ideally with a glass of moscato or any other sparkling dessert wine.

Cornetto, Chifel / Horn Bread

Cornetto is a bread shaped like the French croissant, made with a 00 (doppio zero) flour dough folded to create layers of pastry, much like puff pastry. It is sometimes made with pane all'olio, a dough made with oil or butter to make it more crumbly. A similar bread, called chifel, is made in Trentino-Alto Adige.

Crostini di Pane / Tuscan Toasted Bread

Crostini have recently become very fashionable all over the world. Originally from Tuscany, they are made with slices of unsalted Tuscan bread that is toasted and spread with a pâté of chicken livers, a wild boar ragù or vegetables. Tuscans eat this canapé with aperitifs, but selections with various toppings are now also served as a first course. The finest crostini are spread with a pâté and topped with a slice of truffle.

Farinata / Unleavened Bread

The most ancient methods of making breads used just flour and water, with no raising agent. A wide range of flours, including those of wheat, rye and barley, can be used, but an old and unusual bread that is still made today in Piedmont and more particularly in Liguria, is based on chickpea flour.

Fave dei Morti / Almond Biscuits

On 2 November, Italians celebrate the Day of the Dead. Fave dei morti, which literally translates as 'broad beans of the dead', is the name given to the biscuits eaten during the festival in Piedmont, Lombardy and in many other regions.

Focaccia / Flat Bread

Focaccia is also known as pinza in Veneto, pitta in Calabria, pizza in Naples, pissalandrea in Genova, schiacciata in Emilia-Romagna, fitascetta in Lombardy, sardenaria in Liguria, and stiacciata in Tuscany. Whatever it is called, however, this bread has the same basic characteristics, being a flat bread made with a bread dough (see the basic recipe on page 15) mixed with olive oil and salt. A simple version of focaccia was eaten by the Romans and over the centuries has developed until now there is a multitude of varieties, both salted and sweet, depending on taste and the availability of local ingredients.

Before it is cooked, the dough is pressed flat in the tin and little indentations are made all over with the fingers so that the olive oil that is drizzled abundantly over the dough collects in them to give the dough a wonderful flavour. Coarse salt is then sprinkled sparingly on top and the dough baked until it is golden brown.

Perhaps the tastiest version of them all is the focaccia al formaggio, a speciality of Camogli, an enchanting fisherman's town near Genova. Two very thin layers of dough made of plain flour, water, oil and yeast, are worked in a similar way to strudel dough. The layers are filled with plenty of stracchino cheese, drizzled with olive oil and baked until the cheese has melted.

Frisella, Fresella, Frisedda, Pan Biscotto / Biscuit Bread

Frisella was born of the necessity to create a completely dry bread without moisture that would not be susceptible to mould. It was widely used, first of all, by the army and navy because of its keeping qualities. The bread, made mostly with durum wheat flour, is partially baked then removed from the oven and, while still warm, cut into thick slices or, as with the Campanian and Pugliese frisella, which are shaped like a small ciambella, they are cut in two. The sliced bread is then put back in the oven until all its moisture has evaporated and it has become crisp like a biscuit. Before it is used, it is put under running water for a few seconds so that it is not too hard to eat. It has its own special flavour and is often served with ripe tomatoes, olive oil, salt and basil. Once a favourite snack of farmers, it is now enjoyed by everyone.

Frollino / *Shortcrust Biscuit*
Made with shortcrust pastry (see Pasta Frolla), these biscuits come in various shapes and sizes and are produced and sold all over Italy. They are often eaten dipped into milk and coffee for breakfast.

Gallette / *Biscuit*
This biscuited hard bread is specifically baked for long conservation. It used to be produced for the army and navy, and the only way to eat it was to dip it in water to make it edible.

Grissino / *Breadstick*
Grissini, crisp thin breadsticks made using type 0 flour, water, yeast and sometimes a little olive oil, originally came from Turin but are now eaten all over the world. The long sticks of bread can reach up to 70 cm (28 inches) in length and are still handmade by stretching a piece of dough until it is round and thin before baking it until crispy and dry. To achieve an even more crumbly texture, oil or butter are added to the dough. They are also commercially made and those wrapped in cellophane can keep for many months. *Grissini* can be eaten with any food, but are mostly served with antipasti, or as a substitute for normal bread during a meal. They can also be wrapped in a thin slice of Parma ham to make a delicious snack.

Guastedde / *Sicilian Bread*
This special bread roll is sold filled with a variety of ingredients, but most famously the local delicacy of fried spleen sold at Vucceria market in Palermo. The bread roll is made with a leavened dough of mixed plain and semolina flour, yeast and water, sprinkled with sesame seeds. They are cut in half and filled with the spleen which has been boiled then thinly cut and fried, along with *ciccioli* (pork fat), in lard and spices. The whole thing is then sprinkled with pecorino cheese to make a really wonderful and quite unusual snack.

Maritozzo / *Sweet Roman Bread*
This sweet brioche-type bread is traditionally eaten during Lent in Lazio and Umbria, although today it is available all year round. It is made with a sour dough that requires a long process of proving before ingredients such as eggs, sugar, olive oil and salt are added. The dough is then left to rise again for about four hours, before further kneading and the addition of more ingredients, such as flour, raisins, orange peel, more eggs and a little milk. It can then be divided into small pieces before being baked.

Mostacciolo, Mustazzoli / *Must Biscuits*
One of the most common of the Italian biscuits, *mostacciolo* (or *mustazzoli* in Sicilian) are made and eaten in many regions, although there are usually slight variations on the basic recipe.

The hard dry biscuits, which used to be made by the Ancient Romans, consist of a mixture of plain flour, cooked grape juices (the product of wine-making called must) or honey, and spices like cinnamon, clove and nutmeg; but they do not contain either yeast or eggs.

Pan de Mei, Pan Meino / *Sweet Lombardian Bread*
A small, sweet bread made with a combination of maize and wheat flour, *pan de mei* is typical of Lombardian cuisine.

Pan di Ramerino / *Rosemary Bread*
Pan di Ramerino is a sweet bread traditionally made and eaten at Easter in Tuscany. As the name suggests, the dough includes rosemary oil, together with the more usual sweet ingredients of sugar, raisins and butter.

Pan di San Giuseppe / *Decorative Bread*
This bread, skilfully modelled into a variety of shapes and symbols, is used to decorate altars before being offered to the Holy Family and given to friends as a good omen on

San Giuseppe's day. The bread is a reminder of the legend of the saint, who is celebrated annually with a special meal, *la cena di San Giuseppe* (the supper of St Joseph) in the village of Salemi, a small village built on top of a high hill near Trapani in Sicily.

The story that inspires this celebration is that of a fisherman and his wife who lived in the village. One day, as the fisherman went off on a fishing trip, his wife promised that should he survive his next fishing trip she would invite the entire village to dinner. However, the fisherman and his wife were so poor that when he suddenly returned, all she had to feed to her guests was flour and water, which she made into bread in the shape of the food she would have dearly loved to have given and of Christian symbols.

Pan di Spagna, Pasta Margherita, Pasta Maddalena / Pasta Viennese / *Sponge Cake*
Pan di spagna is a basic soft, sweet sponge cake, made by beating together 6 egg yolks with 250 g (9 oz) caster sugar until you have a foamy mixture. Bake for 30 minutes at 180°C/350°F/gas4, then remove and allow to cool. Cut in half and fill with cream or jam.

Pandolce / *Sweet Bread*
Like *panettone* is for the Milanese, *pandolce* is the centrepiece of the Christmas feast for the Genovese. It

is a much smaller and heavier cake than panettone, as it contains so much candied fruit, raisins and nuts as well as special flavourings like orange water or aniseed. It takes quite a long time to bake, because of the amount of time it takes for the dough to rise.

Pandoró / *Veronese Christmas Cake*
Literally translated, *pandoro* means 'golden bread', because of its deep yellow centre, due at least in part to the number of free-range eggs included in the cake along with 00 (doppio zero) flour, sugar, butter and yeast. It is an extremely light, moist and spongy cake, made by the Veronese and Venetians at Christmas. Due to the lengthy method, taking several days and requiring three proving stages, the Veronese no longer make it at home, preferring to buy commercially made versions. This tall cake is traditionally made in an eight-pointed star-shaped mould. It is usually eaten on its own, although I like it buttered then grilled so that the sugar in it caramelizes slightly.

Pane / *Bread*
One of the basic elements of the Italian diet is bread. Italians eat a great deal of bread on a daily basis, of all types and shapes according to the regional resources of grain and the type of food with which it is to be eaten.

The most common flour used for

breadmaking in Italy is wheat, which is milled to make a very fine white flour. The flour is graded as 00 (doppio zero) and is also used to make, among other things, fresh egg pasta. Slightly less refined flour is graded 0, and so on until wholemeal flour, called *integrale*, containing the husk of the grain. It is, of course, well known that wholemeal flour is more nutritious and is a better source of roughage than white flour, but white flour and white bread are still more popular than the brown in Italy. In southern Italy, 00 (doppio zero) flour is mixed with durum wheat semolina to give the bread a much more solid consistency than the more delicate bread made in other parts of Italy. There are many other flours used to make bread, each of which gives a special quality to the finished product. Other flours used to make bread in Italy include rye, maize and cornflour, which is mixed with white flour for a more developed taste and more digestible bread.

The North prefers very white bread and mostly in small shapes. Liguria prefers *focaccia*, Emilia-Romagna *pane a pasta dura*, a white bread with a hard consistency, and a flat bread called *piadina*. Tuscany has a saltless bread called *pane sciocco*, to accompany its various savoury dishes, salami and spicy preserves. Rome loves the *sfilatino*, a short baguette also called *bastone*, or 'stick'. The entire South is definitely much happier with more substantial bread, like the *pugliese*, which is made of hard durum wheat and keeps fresh for a longer period of time. The round loaves can be gargantuan in size, to satisfy large families.

Special breads are also made using a wide variety of flavouring ingredients, including lard, butter, olive oil, sun-dried tomatoes, herbs, olives, nuts, and a range of seeds.

Because it has to be fresh, bread is mostly bought on a daily basis. This is true especially in the North, because white bread rolls don't keep for more than a day. There are, however, various recipes containing stale bread which is turned into soups, salads and other specialities.

Panettone / *Milanese Christmas Cake*

The most widely made and eaten of the regionally based Christmas cakes in Italy, *panettone* or 'the big bread' is the tallest and largest cake of all; a result of the lengthy procedure required to make it, including many proving periods. It is a difficult cake to make at home because it involves the mixing of two sets of dough – one made with flour, yeast, butter and sugar that needs to prove for about 10 hours, and the other a mixture of flour, butter, eggs, sugar, salt, cubes of candied citron and orange peel, and raisins, which has to be mixed with the first dough and the whole thing left to prove for another 4 or 5

hours. It is then baked in precise, temperature-controlled ovens, which allow the cakes to mushroom up and gently cook until they are dark brown but not burned, leaving the insides wonderfully fluffy and moist. Like the other traditional Christmas cakes, *panettoni* are only baked from October until November.

The most important thing to look for when buying your *panettone* is the quality of the fats used in making it, as this will determine the flavour of the cake. It is also worth checking the date, as the freshest are the best. In response to consumer demands, many cakes are now covered or filled with chocolate or sabayon sauce. However, the simple classic cake is still by far the best.

Panforte / *Fruit and Spice Cake*

This typical Tuscan speciality dates from the Middle Ages, when the first spices were imported from the Mediterranean. Sienna is the city that assumed the paternity of this 'strong bread', which is now quite famous all over the world. See the recipe on page 40.

Parrozzo / *Almond Cake*

A speciality of Pescara in the Marche region, this simple cake is made with flour, eggs, sugar and yeast, enriched with ground almonds and covered with chocolate.

Pasta di Mandorle, Pasta Reale, Marzapane, Marturana / *Marzipan*

A sweet paste based on ground almonds and sugar, marzipan is used by pastry chefs to make cakes and petits fours, and is especially popular in the South and Sicily, where almonds grow in abundance. Another special almond paste called *marturana*, was originally made by nuns in a convent at Marturana in Palermo, Sicily. It is used to make figures and various shapes like fruit and animals, which are then coloured and used to decorate cakes and other desserts.

Pasta Frolla / *Sweet Shortcrust Pastry*

The easiest pastry to make, shortcrust pastry is used in a large number of different types of sweet dishes.

Pasta Sfoglia / *Puff Pastry*

See Prussiani on page 30.

Piadina, Piada / *Romagnan Bread*

This unleavened bread from Emilia-Romagna is similar to the Arabic pitta bread, but tastier. It is usually eaten with the local speciality of Parma ham, stracchino cheese or even sautéed spinach, but may also be served as an accompaniment to other dishes. There are almost as many recipes as there are families who make this bread.

Pissaladeira / Type of Pizza

This *focaccia* covered with anchovies and onions is said by the Genoese to come from *pizza alla Andrea*, after Andrea Doria, the famous Ligurian sailor. It is, however, very similar to *pissaladière*, the savoury tart of neighbouring Provence. See Focaccia, page 15.

Pizza

There are two periods in the history of the pizza: the AP period (Ante Pizza) in which the pizza was considered just a bread to accompany other foods like the Indian naan); and the PP (Post Pizza) period, when toppings were added, leading to the current idea of the pizza being a bread base for any combination of ingredients.

The optimum way of obtaining a good Neapolitan pizza dough is to produce your own sour dough starter. Mix some flour with water to a soft dough and leave this in a warm place for a day. The natural yeasts will have fermented and caused it to rise, so this will be a perfect natural starter for the pizza dough. Alternatively simply use brewer's yeast. See the *pizzette* recipe on page 23.

Pugliese

This term is used to describe a wide range of items made in Puglia, but perhaps nowadays here is mostly used to refer to bread. *Pane Pugliese* is a very large round bread, about 40 cm (16 inches) in diameter and 12-14 cm (5-6 inches) high, with a thick and dark crust. It is made using plain wheat flour with the addition of hard durum wheat flour, resulting in a very dense, wholesome and extremely flavoursome bread, able to last for several days.

Ricciarello / Tuscan Almond Biscuit

See page 35.

Salatini / Little Savouries

All small savoury pastry snacks served with aperitifs are known as *salatini*. They are usually made with puff or shortcrust pastry, topped with cheese, anchovies, capers, olives, or seeds such as those of the poppy and fennel, or simply with ground pepper or salt. You can make these nibbles with frozen puff pastry and the flavouring of your choice, but in Italy they can be bought at the *pasticceria*.

Savoiardo / Sponge Finger

See page 37.

Sfogliatella / Puff Pastry Cake

In Campania and Naples, *sfogliatella* is sold in bars as a rather wonderful snack. They are usually served warm, but are also very good cold. There are two varieties, one a simple pocket of shortcrust pastry and the other a much more elaborate affair involving a special puff pastry, made with a dough of lard instead of butter. The filling usually consists of cooked semolina with ricotta, sugar, eggs, chopped candied peel and a few drops of vanilla essence.

Tarallo, Taralluccio, Tarallino / Round Savoury Biscuit

See page 27.

Zeppola / Choux Pastries

This Southern speciality, usually produced for the celebration of San Giuseppe's Day, is made with eggs, yeast, 00 (doppio zero) flour and lard. The dough, deep-fried in oil, is usually extruded by a syringe, giving a round shape similar to that of *ciambella*. The cooked pastries are then dusted with icing sugar or filled with cream, or even dipped in honey diluted with water to make them absorbent and juicy. My mother used to bake a savoury version, with a piece of anchovy in the middle of the spoonful of dough, which gave an extremely tasty result.

Index

Publishing Director: Anne Furniss
Creative Director: Mary Evans
Editor: Lewis Esson
Consultant Art Director: Helen Lewis
Design: Sue Storey
Cover Design: Claire Peters
Assistant Editor: Jane Middleton
Editorial Assistant: Rhian Bromage
Production: Sarah Neesam &
               Vincent Smith

This edition first published in 2013 by
Quadrille Publishing Limited,
Alhambra House,
27-31 Charing Cross Road,
London WC2H OLS

Based on material originally
published in *Carluccio's Complete
Italian Food.*

Text © 1997 & 1999 Carluccio's
Partnership
Photography © 1997 Estate of
André Martin
Cover Illustrations © 2013
Zack Blanton
Design, edited text and layout ©
1999, 2013 Quadrille Publishing Ltd

Cataloguing-in-Publication Data: a
catalogue record for this book is
available from the British Library.

ISBN 978 184949 484 7

Printed in China.